CITY BIRD AND OTHER POEMS

ALSO BY PATRICK JAMES DUNAGAN

POETRY

There Are People Who Say That Painters Shouldn't Talk: A Gustonbook
(Post-Apollo Press, 2011)
Das Gedichtete (Ugly Duckling, 2013)
from *Book of Kings* (Bird and Beckett, 2015)
Drops of Rain / Drops of Wine (Spuyten Duyvil, 2016)
Sketch of the Artist (FMSBW, 2018)
After the Banished (Empty Bowl, 2022)

CRITICISM

The Duncan Era (Spuyten Duyvil, 2016)

EDITOR

A Walk Among the Bogus by Owen Hill (Lavender Ink, 2014)
Roots & Routes: Poetics at New College (w/ Marina Lazzara
& Nicholas J. Whittington) (Vernon Press, 2020)
Rock Tao by David Meltzer (Lithic, 2022)

CITY LIGHTS SPOTLIGHT SERIES NO. 24

PATRICK JAMES DUNAGAN

CITY BIRD
AND OTHER
POEMS

CITY LIGHTS
SAN FRANCISCO

CITY LIGHTS SPOTLIGHT
The City Lights Spotlight Series was founded in 2009,
and is edited by Garrett Caples.

ISBN 978-0-87286-933-2

Library of Congress Cataloging-in-Publication Data

Names: Dunagan, Patrick James, author.
Title: City bird and other poems / Patrick James Dunagan.
Description: San Francisco : City Lights, 2024. | Series: City Lights spotlight series ; no. 24
Identifiers: LCCN 2024010171 | ISBN 9780872869332 (trade paperback)
Subjects: LCGFT: Poetry.
Classification: LCC PS3604.U497 C58 2024 | DDC 811/.6—dc23/eng/20240307
LC record available at https://lccn.loc.gov/2024010171

Cover art:
Joshua Coffy, *Bird Song #3* [detail] (2015), latex paint on concrete, three stories high.
Located at 1540 Market Street, San Francisco, CA 94102.
Copyright © 2015 by Joshua Coffy, 2023 by the Estate of Joshua Coffy.
Photograph by Garrett Caples.

The editor would like to thank Theresa Summer, Amy Ahlstrom, Joen Madonna,
Micah Ballard, Mary Catherine Kinniburgh, Lee Ranaldo, Kent Johnson,
Peter Maravelis, and Vesuvio Cafe for various forms of assistance.

City Lights Books are published at the City Lights Bookstore,
261 Columbus Avenue, San Francisco, CA 94133
www.citylights.com

FOR AVA

SUPPOSITIONS

Within every sensitive soul (sailor, poet, invalid) there is always
a great ape and a tomb.
—HÉLÈNE CIXOUS

À quoi me sert, bon sang
d'être poète
un peu magicien
selon la rumeur, dompteur de mots
si je n'arrive pas
à inventer, de cette chanson
les paroles?

[What's it mean, damn it
to be poet
near magician
rumored lyre-tamer
if not to
invent today's song
of words]
—ABDELLATIF LAÂBI

You shall soon surrealize that
it requires as much talent
to *live* a poem as to write
a poem.

— TED JOANS

Machines are metal, they serve us, we take care of them. This is
to me, and this is to you. You say you to me, and I say you to you.
Some machines are very delicate, they are precise, they are not big
metal stampers. She made enough poetry to keep her company.

— JOANNE KYGER

Mission, Market, and Van Ness: it is like the beginning of a
poem. Or the end of one.

— R.L. DUFFUS

CONTENTS

CITY BIRD AND OTHER POEMS

CITY BIRD

"Imponderable," Hugh declared,
    delighted, in his
  proclamations ever immersed,
      through anecdote, thoroughly
launching his joy

beyond mere audition.

Sounding off on
    any or every
  possible hushed, occluded
      effort. Channeling his
thoughts, advancing upon

the world passing

round in her
    song. What a
  story resists speaks
      to expected fate.
The desire to

speak of circles

in linear pattern
        developing from out
    hours of repetition,
            progressively limited, partnering
sound with sense,

delving ever deeper.

This outside listening
        tempts those who
    fate allocates shares—
            action undertaken as
anonymous purveyors of

the ancient arts.

Having unexpectedly broken
        in, laid bare
    fresh material, everyday
            realities, those first
recognitions compelling response,

urge present compositions.

Looking back, another
     hour, there is
   another story foretold
      of burnt offerings
left out along

forgotten, rambling stops,

this or that
     mountaintop once thought
   highest, yet now
     recognized as only
numbering among the

tallest peaks earliest

settlers of this
     area took to
   calling *paradise* . . . What's
     been said. Who
knew what and

where: details of

the ongoing job.
　　Observing necessary protocols,
　complete with dotted
　　　"i's" and crossed
"t's," compliant is

how things shall

be filed. Without
　　any hint of
　resolution. Documents withheld
　　　as expected. Next
day the sun

rises and work

commences again, not
　　one bit of
　difference noted. Who
　　it is holding
back, who not,

a question of

non-partnership portending distanced
     allotment. A question
   portrayed as statement
      of fact. There's
only that. Every

ounce of material

asserts it factual.
    Like a cop
  exploring spaced out
     hippie shit, folds
of time prove

intricate. Closer examination

reveals how similar
    our ways are,
  how embedded we've
     grown, our patterns
of thought becoming

alike, mirroring those

among reported accounts.
    Not heading out,
  staying round home
      pondering the next
move. I wonder

as my thoughts

wander. Evoking Wordsworth,
    Whitman, or is
  it Proust, confusing
      recalled readings, even
the imaginary remains

nothing but an

attempt that fails
    escape the all
  too real *real*
      of the real.
Did the missing

text turn up?

All day you
        complained about how
    worried you were.
            What if it
did fall into

nefarious hands? Or

perhaps it is
        simply awaiting your
    return to the
            exact location where
you carelessly dropped

it . . . but where?!?

Turn the radio
        over to hear
    the news above
            his frantic disregard
for respectable amplification.

We've been traveling

together for weeks
    never having before
  spent so much
    time in close
proximity. It's all

so surprising. The

bells begin in
    less than an
  hour. I'll turn
    the radio back
over then and

we'll have that

walk I promised.
    To gather information
  watching light roll
    over sand with
the waves, transforming

instance after instance,

as the waves
  roll back again
 and again. Over
    millennia rocks form
tide pools. Amazing

inconsistency of constant

occurrence. We called
  him *"Toots."* Given
 his tendency to
   blow bubbles which
he then loved

to indiscreetly "p-o-p."

"Just passing the
   time," he called
 it. We loved
   him. His lips
were precious pressure

points of our

markedly shared enthusiasm.
    The workshop slid
  back and forth
      on the slopes
of hilarity, living

and breathing with

circumstantial heft of
    the subjects covered.
  The young are
    eternal and dumb
cuz that's all

they hear. Transmigration,

as Ceravolo knew,
    is needed. What
  you are unable
    to see is
exactly what you

must realize. *Geographical*

maps are such
   beautiful things (Apollinaire)
  How we desire
      truth in fragments.
Timidity is no

vice. The young

fracture the old.
     Pop insisted there
   be rules. He
        brought over some
golden rods offering

them up. If

The House proved
      agreeable they'd have
   an arrangement. When
      I came into
the picture nobody

cared about identity.

I slid back
       into the landscape.
    Witness to everything
           yet refusing fully
take part. Some

calling it criminal

to show up
       like that without
    a hand in
          the game. No
doubt writing is

criminal living. So,

what if star
      dust flows through
    our veins, why
           don't we declare
it? Nothing coheres.

A hard covenant

to live by.

    Doesn't all water

      run together—clouds

        and sky defining

our common everyday

vast amazing variety

conjured irregularly above

      we gaze up

    into. Words just

        some junk stashed

away. The poet

an arranger inquiring

after permanence reflects

      upon mirrored occurrences,

    fragmentary moments: hours,

        minutes, seconds . . . solidified.

Such non-transitory instances

of time during

which each stare
        turns inward, lots
    drawn. We drove
            eight hours southeast
into the desert.

Thoughts of Cezanne's

watery garden settings
        pounding the brain.
    That limitless escape
            hungering, crouching down
in the corner.

Irrepressible. Emptied space

roaring back, lively
        unannounced terror. Directing
    our line of
            inquiry. The road
once taken remains

openly disarming, out

of step. Kerouac's
     American Sideshow notwithstanding.
  We pull off
     forgetting our miasma
lapsing into pit-stop

routine of standard

watering. The poet
     behind this work
  is comfortable moving
     mouths of others.
His or her

ideal reader is

an open value,
     willing intake of
  whatever flows arrive
     beginning the next
shift. Initiating an

ever varying approach

towards—if not
     completion—that which
  by its very
      nature compels incompletion.
Nothing to win,

no goal visualized,

the ongoing pursuit
     left off . . . forgotten
   passages returned to
     late nights, slipping
in & out

of recollection, always

nearly there. *Here*
   you are. Desiring,
  driven by instinct,
    pouncing your way
along. Little difference

between the roaming

cat and that
    lounging gait the
  flâneur flaunts. Whoever
      walks with management
backs into a

corner, no other

choice. Answering for
    others bedevils the
  combing out of
      rats from within
one's self. Allows

entry to clever

types browsing the
    stacks. Who slip
  between rows out
      in the field
at night, the

mist of early

morning but a
        dream in the
    crow's caw. Eye
            gazing interrupts cloud
drift pierced through

with fiery rays

revealing solid blue:
        winter daydreaming out
    the window hinting
            of super powers
squaring off in

forbidden quarters cloistered

away from local
        denizens. Dreams bottom
    out. The urgency
            of inscription mounts.
Vibrant, inescapably startling

tawny owls swarm

round. Eager discussion
ensues. Swans of
serious decorum erupt
in viscous soaring.
There is distinctly

pornographic residual left

on the mantle.
Oil derricks pumping
the earth. Turntables
spinning songs forever
muted. Listed mid-ship

in utter disarray.

.

Clinging garments draped
in jewelry. An
evacuated spirit haunts
the hallowed soul.
No mirage, dependency

offers solace, if

you don't believe
    in being handicapped
  lit-up by emotional
      baggage, i.e., don't
look back. Parts

of wholes, frail

outlines of left
    behind garnishments offering
  no room for
    reflection. Tie back
the ears to

avoid a mess.

Those are stars.
    Pulsations of light
  never to be
    recognized. There is
enough of everything

to go on

forever until there
        isn't. There is
    too much. All
            this everyday counts
down as it

adds up. To

what? The everything
        that is nothing.
    Nothing that is
            what counts. An
applicable measurement of

accrual. That unsaid

which remains said,
        ever present in
    passing hours. A
            daily repetition ad
infinitum. No backing

down or easing

off. No reversing
        course. Endures. That's
    what it does.
            What we do.
What work's about.

Getting up to

have another run
        at it. Following
    unknown trafficking among
            clouds. The sky
above the only

constant, ever-changing. There

are no favorites.
        Favors available only
    at a cost.
            Insufficiency borrowed on
bad luck. This

distrustful one tapping

the other shoulder.
    We end in
  war. Categorical wise-ass—
      exactly what the
doctor didn't know

better than not

to prescribe. Astonished
     citizenry brazenly applaud.
  Sets the room
     into hysterics. Just
another Sunday afternoon

off the quad.

All church services
    move outdoors for
  summer. In the
    heat, the choir
cuts things short

by a song

or two. Hugh
          bites in. The
     only thing he
          truly understands how
do well. His

life always the

memory of a
          performance he fails
     show for. "Oh
          well," he tells
himself, "got to

keep on moving."

Glumly, but not
          without a certain
     amount of pure
          unhindered joy, chomping
away. Dead-eyed lines

met with expected

results. While the
     moment passes holding
  on entails grasping
     after fading mirages.
Past recollections of

future division jam

our siloed communications.
     What brings end
  to infinite expansion.
     Words don't beat
sorrow. Once the

heart collapses nothing

reasonable serves fill
     vacant chambers. Another
  opportunity to pass
     into the void.
There's nothing gets

done. It must

be stressed inadequacy
      remains our strongest
   suit against powers
      that be. We
are inherently inadequate

tools for accomplishing

anything. Inert. That
   is our greatest
  strength. Those who
     are adequate shall
fail. The streets

tonight are loud

with support for
   failure. For now
  we rest accomplished
    in our tomorrows.
Only the most

dangerous sort of

whimsical frolic draws
     us out from
   our s(h)elves. Men
      are robust. Women
meek. How lessons

have failed us.

Ah, yes, how
     lessons fail us.
   Judged to be
     nibbling the edges
feels indefensibly unfair

as if being

fragmentary were optional.
    That always imminent
   threat that nothing
     no matter what
will be good

enough. Only extremities

offer passage. Although
    never entirely safe
  or very pleasant
    with kooks lurking
every-which-ever path you

turn down. Place

the tokens down
    before you, however,
  and you shall
    not be blocked.
Magic frequently serves

answer during perilous

moments of doubt.
    The young always
  most approachable yet
    there is need
throughout our lives

for the hope

the miraculous offers
     from out darkness.
   To ward off
      cross-cultural curses wide-spread
belief says we

have far more

good in us
     than conceivably possible.
   You all are
     a dark lot.
All this comes

soaring along standing

on some corner
     under average sky
   one afternoon. Makes
      you wonder what
larger forces at

work beyond our

ken continually shape
and re-shape the
hours of our
lives. What answers
lie buried beneath

such sap we're

never willing peel
back bark to
extricate. Patriotism. What
a bag. "Horseshit."
Hugh calls it,

mumbling to himself.

Shit on My
Shoes. Under another
name. Self-interested prick.
"It's you and
me, Kid." All

that loose, sentimental

crap. The game
     is fixed. Don't
  any you fuckers
      doubt it, snot-nosed
and unworthy, carry

on! No anecdote

is worth preserving.
     I did this.
     I did that.
       The voices are
telling you exactly

what needs saying

if you will
     listen. The job
  is a snake.
       Such lonesome sighs
driven straight out

of town ending

up here. Book
     on besting assholes
  and you just
      might pull it
off. The rest

of us fade

out in red
     forever young except
  we're actually growing
     older all this
time. Listen, when

you're gone, you're

gone. Every moment
     presents a fresh
  memory precise as
     any other. How
exactly does this

happen. Strange but

not exotic thoughts
             cloud the mind,
        always have far
                  back as memory
reaches. Timeless hours,

days spent strolling

streets at random
             map checking only
        to retain such
                  roughly sketched out
trajectory ensures some

sense of capable

return remains certain.
             Stirring the work
        of living into
                  action. Taking heart
in wandering spaces

unfamiliar. Embrace any

discomfort, detest only
what you full
well recognize easily
as the door
of one's own

home. There is

territory and then
there is territory.
Map is our
territory in one
case but may

not be hung

dependably upon in
the next. Whenever
you are mappable
you are immigrant.
The world hostile.

Tread with care.

At another turn
       the sky bleeds
    out ink and
           as ground gives
way substance swallows

you limb-by-limb. You

have reached beyond
       the map. Exchanges
    made by the
           hour. How in
back of his

mind he lurked

round the room
       in the rear
    submersed within business,
           requesting variance for
having another sector

assigned to him.

Encrypted German or
      something but nothing
   deceitful seemingly, if
      nothing true. Spelling
always arising as

an issue. Whether

any of this
      is understood as
   intended. What is
      the word you
wanted? Desire is

only as useful

as any other
      instrument. Letting the
   nose lead as
      one would if
it were a

dog's, tail and

all, that you
            followed. Careful not
       to overwork it.
                 Afforded brief respite
a few of

us linger in

the cooling lean-to
          obliged carry on
       into The West
               with our cargo.
I'm back out

checking threats, the

outlandish wetness of
        his tongue tracing
      final remains left
            out in the
open to be

discovered. There is

nothing funny about
    this but I'm
  laughing all the
      same. Under Norma's
window Brian's creeping

about. The lights

are on but
    nobody's to be
  seen. This is
      spirit talk. Wishing
for the best

employing glass clear
    rather than fuzzy
  blurred round the
      signature "ring of
fire" found bottom

of older bottles.

A whole year
    circling her block
  at least once
      a week yet
you never noticed.

Hold the results,

we'll need evidence
        to get us
    out of this
            fix. Transactional proof
alone matters. Although

as much as

it matters, things
        remain as they
    are, lost to
            us forever. Familiar
hangers-on, those words

left with mouths

hanging open in
        state of pure
    anticipation. How it
            feels to know
every part, yet

not be part

of the whole.

    Asked about it,

  you have no

      qualms in answering

affirmatively, "These are

those among many

you have sought

    for in vain."

  Simple as that.

      Turning the table

to position the

next questioner under

that same red

    moon in the

  dead of a

      winter night. Every

wish the larger

world resists. One

continuous fabric tussled
with against the
necessary reality some
call Angel and
others Devil. Follow

the light to

the end of
that pier, dazzling
crystalline sheen extending
out below, pop-n-flow
of jetsam, harbor

trash really, banging

against pilings. His
memory the writing
continues. We're approaching
being there. Creeping
closer every which

way and we're

not going to
      be looking back.
    Plowing ahead. What
       a mélange! This
gang of words

driven through the

head. Murder of
      crows flapping round
    roof-peaks cawing into
       the morning air.
I'll wake with

scattered ink and

watch how they
      soar about above
    the street out
       front. Bestowed radiance,
the coming light

gently rising from

off hilltops as
            the cars swing
        up. Activity in
                the street, trains
and cars sharing

the middle lanes.

That passing pedestrian
            the sidewalk grimaces
        under. All the
                hustle of fabricated
thoroughfares, how useless.

Our agendas reshape

nothing—never have.
            Each hour has
        its own momentum.
                Feel it. Don't
ruin yourself, reaching

for it. Outside

thought of beginning
    to write arouses
  the impulse to
      write. Nothing describes
the actual momentary

occasion better than

the absence of
    it. Forgotten dinners
  long ago missed
      due to excessive
drinks & much

talk beforehand. The

compulsions to keep
    going. Reading each
  endeavor after the
      next into coming
action ahead. She

gave her feedback

as calmly as
        an overabundant amount
    of aggressively feeling
            WTF allowed for.
These gatherings are

so sobering yet

nobody leaves early.
        Just being there
    is as lovely
            an occasion as
possible given the

situation outside. I

heard he bowled
        well, so I
    took him at
            his word: complete.

Exchanging sensitive glances

of like-measured estimation
      over who bests
   who when words
      are torn away.
Trading on losses.

Lots assigned at

terminus. No easy
      passing back and
   forth between cars
      although there's plenty
gauge ahead not

giving us too

much trouble. Is
      it Broken Vowel
   Syndrome? Maybe, hard
      to say, but
maybe. You see

Jimmy pushes us

so hard we
        hardly would have
        heard of anything
                like that round
here. Just like

Heaven, or The

Apocalypse: two sides
        of one outlook,
        each no weightier
                than the other,
or less bleak, await.

A celestial parlor

game for kicks.
        Comes down to
        mere numbers, cast
                down in the
back lot, shit

out of luck.

Borrowed breezes arriving
        off morning fogbank.
    A passion for
        all things Greek,
even the scent

in the air

nights after massacres,
        or mass drowning
    cast up against
        the rocks. Notches
in the plank

tallied up. That

silence of coin
        palmed across waters.
    You can't tell
        it anything. Anonymity
gathering in globs.

Mass of pages

piling up. Where
        the ink sets
    down doesn't necessarily
            serve as counterpoint.
Seeking words to

live by, words

her afternoon airs
        took turns reciting.
    Note the lilting
            casual delivery of
her proclamations. Joy

rising up crashes

against the glare
        from front windows.
    No simple high.
            A new alphabet
would be a

good idea but

who would draw
      numbers for all
    those characters? Continue
     working long enough
it grows into

a monumental bulk.

How not discover
     some value buried
   in there somewhere.
      Mess of steady
measured accumulation. Easier

said than done.

It goes away.
     Imagination unravels. Passing
   through streets leaving
     some pieces here
or some bits

over there. A

trail of decomposition.
     Silent wandering hunks
   of material bonded
      together resolutely feeling
their way around

town. Nothing stranger

than seeing them
     traipsing around without
   a sound. Dodgy
     as their appearance
indeed is, there

is no eagerness

among citizens to
     relate with them.
   An unwelcome coolness
     characterizes the reception
fate holds. With

plenty of work

undone and only
          the final quarter
     left these final
               minutes either prove
noteworthy or simply

disappoint. How the

thing grows on
          you, the longer
     you stare the
               steadier the gaze
answers you back.

The work falls

away, unwinds the
          clock facing the
     door not expecting
               be left out
why would you?

No visitors due

stare about awhile
    feeling the walls
  give back sense
     beyond ideas—vision.
Road-less wisdom unasked.

Experience imposes rules

breaking against impulsive
    habit. Listen, just
  sit there. Here
    come the words.
Everybody writing stories

about others. Inconsistent

facts, doing away
    with the freedom
  of open air. Swirling
    tide pools water
gathers round rocks,

danger ever present

risk of just being
    where one's presence
is precarious. He
      even eats teeth.
He could talk

with a wall

and get it
    to respond. Advice
is anything other
    than necessary or
simple enough to

acquire during times

of struggle. Indecision
    never less than
troublesome. She drops
    the iron and
stares. Ignition triggers

the heart, lifting,

by way of
        the blood of
    touch. To launch
            the eye. Something
alien. Something nearer

to the heart.

Hard numbers handed
            over in lines
        of tens keep
            you counting. Oh,
I would never

publish that. Another

sounding out, another
        excelling disavowal of
    the tendency expressed.
            Have a start
at ending. Worked

over remains scattered

just ever so.

      That haranguing is
   constant with him.

         A relentless pushing
at others, to

expose what is

never there in
      the first place.
   that empty script
      in his head
rolls on forever

as he thumbs

through it over
     & over. Wasted
   pornography of unheralded
      depths, blown. Having
targets won't do.

You listen, see,

but don't stop
    to listen, unless
  you forget. Moves
      must arrive in
unison or nothing

moves. Complications compel

desire. Fitting the
    parameters sought after
  he delivers shape
      without comment, broadening
the horizon lines

for us all.

That moment when
    you only know
  of arriving. Proof
      demanding no countenance.
One bowl exchanged

for bowler hat.

Comb given over
    to the comber.
  Trickster denying the
     trick. Practitioner of
the art of

practice. The word

for it. Bent
    design. What Troublesome
  bore. Such diligent
     erasure. Returned uneaten
the whole strikes

the calendar clean.

No blowback. Sticking
    to the strict
  policy keeps them
     returning. Blocks away
the wind still

blows leaves, scatters

trashcans the boy
        will catapult over
    board beneath his
            feet, a wildness
the wheels deliver

to his heart.

Deeply peculiar need
        that will know
    no satisfaction. From
            the lives of
others we draw

understanding. With passion

comes the allure
        of belonging. We
    pass away without
            care dare we
ignore the endless

draw once we've

become aware. A
     friend at the
   center of every
      one of us
reaches out to

the lonely mind

with stubborn tenacity.
     Give us the
   words to obey.
      Write the script
the sky wept.

Do not fail

finish. I listen
     intently to the
   discussion, feeling the
      depth of the
comradery crisp in

the air, realizing

there is nothing
        finer than the
    feeling comes from
            belonging. Hugh settles
in, turning back

to his sandwich.

FOR JOAN BROWN

Artists of California
arrogant and young, destitute in work searching
to have something to say
painting your way out the same situation for years
you guys mock each other what fluffy puppies
the struggle is not to age your age
just maintain number as symbol or sign
age you refuse represent or embody simple
isn't it art to walk away
don't speak out against struggles you don't get
the job isn't to make it but to make things make it
and that job is years in coming
if then you find me riding in a Cadillac
understand it ain't mine at all but possibly
and then typically so unlikely the driver may very well be
slipping between sedimentary levels for sentiment
give such grapple to hold the night through
a cartwheel to drive the draydel
big cats on furry lounges to tempt us
harmony in the background just like that
lettme hearya now!

DELIBERACY

In America it is always high noon. — RICHARD OWENS

I wanna talk over Donald Justice and J.H. Prynne
merits of each without bothering credentials
we wrote that whole book of poems showing you it was easy
start up a rectitudinous school only to later wreck it
bumps in the dust all that's left our frivolous hours
walking a cloudy wave with Samuel Clemens—how he never
blasted with the coolness of a clown
night driving to park outside 24hr conveniences
exchanging no words at all one paltry motherfucker for friend
near enough to share a smoke though hardly there
get this hellcat his rag he's finished
you know your number's up don't feel duped
dos and don'ts sought despite coded gates cave in parties
Blinko your friendliest of hosts has no fears about going back
against staggering loss the dead want nothing to do with
this centaur kid dehydrates outside his spaceship townhouse
universal ads for our steroid powered present
I find it all so literary and great I never dream of leaving

(reading *the truck darling poems*, *sous les paves* #3, and listening to
        the day's news)

MISTAKING IDENTITY'S GRAVITY

under my rising sign—Leo—I think—or is it
Ferdinand, the prince asleep in the waves
—FILIP MARINOVICH

See there's this alien
feeling it may be wrong
              thinking everything's fine when
        really it's impossible understanding
whether knowledge comes of thought or is
  image just another abstraction forgot along-
                        side others
                    what might remain
                        is perhaps too much
                    or simply what's left
        after might's right has darkly rung
        drawing out the whole night's light
        without enough stashed away
        nothing to keep going
        a final bit of longing cranks out with a blast
        from the back pocket of this last minute
        another hour's worth or so
        until feeling fine enough to leave—
                        if only it had been him who
answered the door

THE JOURNAL

I wanted it to be direct and
also to mean quite a lot. I wrote
the story down as it occurred and the
story began to change my words
as I wrote. By the time I contemplated
the first portion of the work
a few years had passed silently by

and several relationships swam through.
I had established my use of incantation
in both modes of living and writing.
I began to witness the acts of the story
occur around me as I had written them.
I realized I was living out the very act I
had spoken of: in the writing, the living.

Prior to this time I had never considered
such development possible. It came
as a contemplative shock, unasked. Yesterday
I began a new chapter. I retain high hopes
that the form will confine all dangers in matters
of instruction, a proper grammar and punctuation.
It is my hope that such will holds.

Walking up O'Farrell it really isn't so bad
a fierce wind blows about your hair
you feel vulnerable unable to despair

hundreds walk with you you feel them in the air
hundreds of hearts hundreds of walks
hundreds of heads with hundreds of thoughts

in the instant the one you love fails to love you back
you figure you'll never know love again any other way
and then you do and everything's okay

SIXES AND TENS

The Sumerians were smart enough to combine sixes and tens
Their year was exact, their poetry
Who knows if their poetry scanned?
—PHILIP WHALEN

Urine-stained volumes, pages crisp curves
cheesy feeling to have the books here, image there
hazards—proof of having gone after the always receding,
phrases knocking bout the head, what for?
    nothing utilized : nothing gained

        self-definition, call it copulation
not "combination," like forms take to like
air of invention? Holds or doesn't
no bother caring
no getting round what's thought

aphorisms for those coming later
drunk in mood of innuendo caught up in countless whodunit
    scenarios
expenses of massive toil
to what point?

Yes, it figures that you'd figure I'd figure to,
so please don't.

All unholy gazooks
poking your way into the scene when you might as well just launch
out
that terrible bother of entertaining visitors

just stop it.

TWENTY-FIVE FOR LEW WELCH

Then they want the rest of us to die for it, too. — LEW WELCH, "The Basic Con"

I've been reading Lew Welch for some 20-odd years. First I read Edgar Allen Poe, Allen Ginsberg, Walt Whitman, Hawthorne, Thoreau, et al.; then I found out about Kenneth Rexroth, Gary Snyder, and Lew Welch. (I heard of Philip Whalen, too, but he took a while longer for me to dig.)

. . .

Welch met Whalen and Snyder when they all were students together @ Reed College in Portland, on lawns where I once threw a Frisbee (was it?) several years ago with my pal Jeffrey Karl Butler and his son Austin. (And then a couple years later went back to see the Jess show.) Lately, I've been avoiding phone calls. I only talk to my mom. I owe Jeffrey up in PDX a good long chat one of these days.

. . .

When I read Lew Welch I often think about Robinson Jeffers (and vice versa)

"I am Roan Stallion"
—Lew Welch

• • •

Both Leos, we're born August 16th

Sunnylyn Thibodeaux, Lew Welch, and me.

• • •

"You know Lew always CRIES when he reads and it will ruin the
     evening."
—JOANNE KYGER

• • •

David Highsmith gave me a broadside for my birthday one year:

RAID KILLS BUGS DEAD

It's up in our bathroom. This tag-line, ad copy throwaway, now embla-
zoned in millions of modern-day minds, is attributed to Welch from
his 9–5 Chicago workadays.

• • •

Huey Lewis, of Huey Lewis and the News, is Welch's step-son. He sang Welch's "Graffiti" with his mother in the audience @ SF Public Library. *Dig it, the Poet sd.*

. . .

In 1971, Welch walked off with his gun never to be seen again.

. . .

Tall and lanky with a bursting head of red, describes Lew Welch if he was a good-looking woman.

. . .

Before any poet bothers to write a poem concerning problems of rat infestation they should be familiar with Welch's "Buddhist Bard Turns Rat Slayer" especially if they consider themselves to be Buddhist and are a "professor" at the University of San Francisco.

. . .

There are moments in Welch's poetry I find him to be the greatest of poets and others where I have no feeling whatsoever for what he's doing.

・ ・ ・

Kush of Cloud House is the biggest fan of Welch I know. Ask him to sing Lew Welch poems for you!

・ ・ ・

One time I wrote and published some sophomoric lines mimicking Welch's "Ring of Bone." *... I saw myself ... in the Dutch stream of her thighs ...*

・ ・ ・

In that photo out of Lisa Jarnot's Robert Duncan biography that's not a bearded (?!?) Welch standing back of a phenomenally drunk looking Jack Spicer next to an elegantly young knockout Joanne Kyger, it's the infamously great poet Ebbe Borregaard!

・ ・ ・

How did she get all the way up this hill
With one leg in a cast
On crutches
Dead drunk
In that very modern party dress
1:30 a.m.

Dirt trail treacherous with Eucalyptus nuts
The night moonless and fogged over anyway?
—WELCH, "For a Kyger Known by Another Name"

• • •

As a young man Welch was among the earliest, as well as by far the most readable and enlightening, of Gertrude Stein scholars.

• • •

There was a riot down off Market St. in San Francisco. Welch went to check it out with Ted Berrigan and Alice Notley. Outside a bar they nearly tripped over Philip Whalen who was drying out his feet, resting them on the unusually sun-warmed pavement. "Hi, Phil," said Notley stooping down as Welch & Berrigan went inside the bar each for a piss and beer.

• • •

In his interview with David Meltzer, Welch identifies Charles Parker and Jack Spicer as the two men most hellbent on self-destruction he'd ever witnessed.

• • •

My great uncle Jack Pinkham lived in San Francisco during the Sixties with his wife Mimi in a large industrial space over near Potrero with his art studio on the roof next to a garden. Their space was the top quarters of a glass manufacturer. My mother would occasionally visit them there before her marriage to my father. She would sit and discuss the Bible with Jack. Lew Welch on occasion picked her up in his cab after she'd been walking the bay's edge for a couple hours and took her back to Jack's. He dug the rooftop garden and all Jack's sculptures scattered about.

• • •

Slang envelops Welch's poems without ever diminishing them.

• • •

My mom and dad used to drive around in RVs. Once they drove up to San Francisco from Anaheim to see her uncle Jack and also pal around with Welch. They went to the river and Welch and my dad sat around smoking pot and drinking whiskey shooting at ground squirrels with a .22 and a bb gun. Both of them broke down in tears when they killed a squirrel.

• • •

Once my dad used a machete to lop off the head of a rattler who had curled up beneath his girlfriend's sweater which she had left under her cot while camping next to the Colorado River. He grilled up the snake and ate it: "Like chicken."

•   •   •

John Cusack recently starred as Edgar Allen Poe in *The Raven*. A horribly confused murder mystery suspense that switched up biographical facts with Poe's fiction and poems. (In the universe of the film Poe's literary executor and subsequent posthumous arch-nemesis Griswold ends up being one of the victims, killed therefore before Poe's own death.) I hope nobody ever makes a film about Lew Welch, or attempts otherwise portray him: this does mean YOU, James Franco. (I do however still hold out hope for the making of the film *POUND*. Sofia Coppola to direct. Sean Penn, nicely wizened, in the lead role. Feeding feral cats, appearing stoic. Lots of silent long shots of sky water earth.)

•   •   •

I've never read Welch's incomplete novel *I, Leo*. Yet have consumed everything else on multiple occasions. Welch's letters are fantastic.

•   •   •

Lew Welch on the ridge breaking dawn corduroy & rifle glistening eye'd gazes down.

OCT. 2012

FOR FELLOW 8/16 LEO IMMORTAL JAMES DENIO

LULLABY

My father changed his habit
I followed him
nightly down the blocks

his route took
became an ever-increasing mess
of dead ends

reversals
changes made at random
I lost him

only to find him
casting about
chasing his own dead ends

once I searched him out
he'd slip free
never one to be cornered

his paths led
to doom
swallowing him

nightly I follow
he's gone
I'm watching him go

DESTROY A LITTLE TO BUILD A LITTLE

Jay DeFeo talked skater
Thrasher woulda' interviewed her

TeD: how's yr art?
JDF: how's yr ass? I threw it all away
purposively

TeD: we appreciate that
JDF: you better

The parks we have now
are DeFeo parks
all those long looping curves
bitterly concluded pipe-dream ends

that's pure DeFeo

as is
the natural impulse

to look at some ledge
or rail

with the urge
to go at it

natural as anything

JEAN ARP, MAR. 1960

Enter the grand universe of night fading
from twilight, born of imagination, awaken
when the cock strikes up his chant, the
cast-off shelf-monsters of Louise Nevelson
walk.
Here are Greeks (Greek Land)
—land of boards swept to shelves
where hope vanishes right out
devastating you.
Here are plain plaints of air
a wandering vast library
a muscular cocoon
a continuous flood of shade
a stack of managed criminal cases.
To awaken as if the flap of dawn,
set against eastern ruins
with honor, its rushing mass, your burial.
At such gates how many of us find ourselves
(the inner gates) passing for an entrance of sorts
such noble beings, such notable individualities.
When else does a drunken bottle elicit
sense of catacomb dust?
The boy-with-the-bags (the wedding chest)

juggles bras, he is despondent looking for the cathedral.
Louise Nevelson is one free motherfucker troubles flee from
for instance, Kurt Schwitters.

AFTER READING MAX JACOB

That excitement come of joy
　　for being so lost

　　　　luxurious illusion embraced
　　made Real in the momentary

　　　　Yes! Yes! friendly with a laugh

another tanker against sunset & tide low
　　　　　　lumbering out into the Pacific

　　at mercy of no god other than Nature

　　　　I believe in religion like magic
　　like science religion to save
　　　　　　the planet our souls but one soul

　　　belief in whatever suits
　　isn't the problem belief slips away
　　　　　　too easily caricatured
(back to the poem
　　　　　lit up under these pines across from the beach
　　aglow resonating highlights all

nothing's better than the Pacific at sundown
wisdom *is* the Sun
some bistro youth vanishes into where
all at once I came upon Love
a long avenue convincingly lit as if forever

the addition of yet another station which we approach
with the tide low penitent while flies refuse leave us be

9/21/21

FOR PETER BOYLE

LILT; LIT: BUILT TO ROLL, DOINGS

In dusk baby calves look like small dogs or wolves
hustling up hilltops to heifer mommas
train zooming across Nebraska night
Omaha day looming American boomtown
idea of the old is new everywhere
miles of roadways enticing genX-er duds
alike post-Depression tykes decades folded
back at glimpse-intervals marking out the path
forward

AFTER DAVID SHAPIRO AFTER FRANK O'HARA

Poetry is doubtful joy
why bother
toning the body
for future use is useless
death lurks every look
you give less than another gives
death lurks every look

go back & forget it
no joy of walking streets
wind batting 'bout the hand
looks round gathering memories
all the talks & drinks gone
let it all go   why not
'til you remember & cling forever

SELF-INTERVIEW

I find in
my writing
the loveliest
sense
of diverse
approaches
& styles
which are
inexplicably
absent from
most others
why
that is
the case I
really
am not
able to
say

BILL BERKSON

Speaking in the 8th person
how you do
giving 5th dimensional testimonial
you vanished in a nanosecond
several vases suffered shattering fates
the General she guffawed
lacking grace you see
the yard suddenly less than inviting
Connie now gone you never to reappear
Kevin gone as well
an ever-narrowing party
slips here to there about town
hopes you smile somehow
somewhere we aren't
may this world you left
welcome a future you'd enjoy
as much as we enjoy
the vessel left behind

ANONYMITY

You don't think about your audience when you're writing. —THOM GUNN

This particular late summer afternoon
an unsettled and unsettling nervousness
bleak tense edgy committed to with brute energy
like having good or bad looks there's nothing to be done
if it comes back it comes back
I really don't care if I cared I'd stop
no tradition that's particular or desirable
everybody so miserable with the burden
this will sound like vanity but it isn't
being recognized right away just inside the door
first by one and then all the rest at the table
in public the chore becomes one of management
say a belief in god is no longer much use
rather the possibility of ghosts
that one good party I've ever attended
no one to recognize me nobody to recognize

INCISION

Do you ever feel
like Han Solo?
Jay DeFeo's?
Nah, just
regular ole blaster-toting Han
cocky arrogant
sometime do-gooding
don't we all?
some leaves dripping damn water all over
loving to be out in it like this
guessing our way
outmaneuvering any bad luck
not too tall really yet
none too short
the beach answers
having our back
drawing out as it flings us
handing out fates the deck
stacked for or against not mattering
fated or not slipping through
listen to the crows hustle
marks showing the way
sandy tracks
down coast

ST. ANNE OF THE SUNSET

One whispering tales of woe to another
cow as heavenly gargoyle
spring dazzler in mystic's ear
boy wonder an island misplaced
tracing hieroglyphic in gypsy blood
all lined up atop Anne's place

SNARL'D

I sat on the steps

  for there were no gondolas
 no water
and it was the wrong time of year anyhow for water taxiing

   altho from the sun's warmth
  you wldn't know it

    Van Ness traffic on a Sunday even
   never a surprise

    tomorrow I head south
  wrapping the years up

    fields flapping past
   as only fast-walking legs manage
    the distances between a conversation
 lagging far behind

    pot-boiler family affairs need tending

the tense lacks substance
　　　　the subject slides all around

winter's ending
　　　where it all began

　　　suburban maze of a young boy's eyes
　　heralding the years yet to come

FOR RICHARD TAGETT @ 80

FEB 14, 2016

BEYOND REACH

In impossible realms
tattooed virgins Melville knew of
work out the literature blues
mouthing their names for each other
one is Wisdom Wrong another Paralyzed Perfect
I let them mess with my hair
this took place centuries ago
I had brought Homer along
his rudimentary charm & dialogue
went over big with the little ones
having withheld the story for so long
I'm pleased it's now coming out
I have put away my sorrow
tattooed virgins Melville knew of
glad I brought Homer along
his chants, the dance continues

IN THE SEACOAST STATES

I go after you like whiskey
refusing to hear your no, your body
a splash of shine
I go after without wishing
I grab after your disappearing heels
because I must remember
I go after blankets of time
drawn around you, your release,
I go after bee-like, zipping along
'til there is a secret, a dry tomb
and no one hears the complaint,
wrecking only an interior drone
silent outside your knowledge
and you are not aware.

I go after my own mountains,
my own affairs
compelling state of habits
playing at my nerves,
I go after your closed eyes,
ears and mind, blinded
I go after what I must, driven,
your lack of books, paintings, music

I am alone, it is my pride
and when you choose turn to look
it is without shine.

RIVER CROSSING

Finally there are no heroes.
The heart keeps up for a while,
hoping for the best, producing all this bullshit.
When you're older you want to do something,
to matter like a leaf shaking on a tree.
He split with 4 bucks and nowhere to go.
Told the dungeons were at 800 feet
his past could not fix him, tie him to any landscape.
Now that I'm through with wishing different
I just want to keep going with it.
The journey is simple. It is the same
rungs of the ladder I must climb.
His nose usually in a book
his affectation merely the result of habit & self-persuasion.
The other side shows exactly how the way back will appear.
I'm being intentionally vague
domination is the name of the game.
Point of departure towards an acceptable version
his moral compass failing him
opening spaces inside you believe yours,
a driver of sorts, his wandering ways.
There's nobody I want to be
having been here and made it back.

SO, SEE

There is this young coyote I've come across a few times now early
mornings as he slopes his way across a relatively wide-open space
between low lying shrubs and lawn to the west with the beginning
of the small oak hills walk to the east, Fulton borders the area to the
north and the large smooth asphalt roller skating pad is immediately
south. He's a nonchalant cool ass cat with nice coloring shades of dark
grey rubbed with smatches of brown. His movement is of deliberate
casualness. He has always been at the table with the poets and artists
and he will always be there. He doesn't say much but we feel all the
cooler for the company. Lucky us.

NOV 17, 2021

READING THOMAS VAUGHN LISTENING
TO MERLE HAGGARD

Having no background to follow let alone allow for but facts of reflec-
tion mirrored by original farmed out in the well of imagination arise
before we've taken time to consider an hour's or more worth of events
parsed throughout tasting liberty come off celestial flowers pasted
down as if what were appears from derivations from apparent iden-
tity's acceptable upon unawareness flows from out folds each brings
experience into her role his most of all yet misunderstood often
tumbles folded in without choice decisions following actions moving
through the walk an exit is to return glimpsed without prejudiced eye
to have been experience all along you have only to compare what's
written with what's heard in yourself the answers which ask am I
going against

e.g.   the

whole entire fold   (so calld

urges its own   being

to realize itself   plots

necessary points of meeting

in so that

                you would have numbers   running up against
        themselves   to sound   out a shade
            others   swirling   no
              things   identities
                        husks of sound
                            what's the time?
              rummaging   old tunes
                    coming & going   with the air

        back of the rock
    the rock become a whale
        the whale tearing down the vale

A WESTERN

John Wayne breaks the heart; a solid wall of ass.
Those "blue suede shoes" pissing where he pleases.
A man turns and runs from such encounters

•

"It was a wilderness and now it's a garden"
Talking to her "choice"
It was her, placed that cactus bloom.

•

In the wrong, Jeff makes it with Kellie.
Kellie makes it with Jeff, in the right.
Kellie and Jeff make it and that's terrific!

•

Tom never got to "make it" with her.
The West never stood a chance.
"Wild," "head over heels," falling flat on your face.

•

"This matter . . . has come to such a pass . . . we must turn bullies"
To begin to end, a "National Literature,"
What I need is three good lines.

MAR 1, 1999

ACKNOWLEDGMENTS

Some of these things previously appeared in the following publications: *1913: A Journal of Forms, Blue Book, HTMLGiant, Lightning'd Press House Mag, Morning Train, The Night Palace, Easy Eden* (PUSH press), *sous les pavés, Volt,* and *Weigh Station.*

Many thanks to all the editors & publishers who have supported my work over the years, especially M.C. Fujiwara, Josh Filan, Kevin Opstedal, Micah Ballard, Jeff Butler, Sunnylyn Thibodeaux, Jason Morris, Julien Poirier, Nicholas James Whittington, & Garrett Caples, editor of the book now in hand, true shaper of its nature and content.

Both debt & gratitude are eternal: In "the poems" *Onward.*

The state of the world calls out for poetry
to save it. LAWRENCE FERLINGHETTI

CITY LIGHTS SPOTLIGHT SHINES A LIGHT ON THE WEALTH
OF INNOVATIVE AMERICAN POETRY BEING WRITTEN TODAY.
WE PUBLISH ACCOMPLISHED FIGURES KNOWN IN THE
POETRY COMMUNITY AS WELL AS YOUNG EMERGING POETS,
USING THE CULTURAL VISIBILITY OF CITY LIGHTS TO BRING
THEIR WORK TO A WIDER AUDIENCE. IN DOING SO, WE ALSO
HOPE TO DRAW ATTENTION TO THOSE SMALL PRESSES
PUBLISHING SUCH AUTHORS. WITH CITY LIGHTS SPOTLIGHT,
WE WILL MAINTAIN OUR STANDARD OF INNOVATION AND INCLUSIVENESS
BY PUBLISHING HIGHLY ORIGINAL POETRY
FROM ACROSS THE CULTURAL SPECTRUM, REFLECTING
OUR LONGSTANDING COMMITMENT TO THIS MOST
ANCIENT AND STUBBORNLY ENDURING FORM OF ART.

CITY LIGHTS SPOTLIGHT